Self-Editing for Writers

By

Ann Jacobs

Tips for Taking Your Book
from Rough Draft to Polished Final

How to Take Your Rough Draft and Polish It for Others' Eyes

Ann Jacobs, multi-published author of bestselling, award-winning novels and novellas, takes you step by step through the self-edits you need to perform before presenting your book or novella to a publisher, a private line editor or the world in general.

- ✓ Maximize the functionality of your word processor to help clean your manuscript while recognizing its limitations

- ✓ Realize where your skills lie when it comes to grammar, punctuation, spelling and word choice, and tailor your self-editing process to account for your strengths—and mitigate your areas of weakness (in other words, where to focus your self-editing efforts to best advantage)

- ✓ Learn to recognize when your manuscript is as good as you can make it—before turning it in to be judged/contracted/presented to the end purchaser

Self-Editing for Writers
is published by Ann Josephson
www.annjacobs.net

Copyright @ 2015 by Ann Jacobs
Cover design by Syneca, ORIGINALSYN
Graphic Design
Edited by Jerald Josephson
Format by Wizards in Publishing

Contents

Section I

Introduction

One day when I was helping to proofread novellas for an anthology, I discovered that, while a writer of popular fiction doesn't need to have earned a Ph.D. in English Grammar and Composition, he or she does need to perform a few simple self-editing functions in order to create works that will aid, not detract from readers' ability to become engrossed in a compelling story line.

The idea for this short, simple guide to self-editing sprang from my experience that weekend. No, I do not have a Ph.D. or even a bachelor's degree in English grammar and composition, creative writing, or any closely related field. My academic credentials consist only of a four-year degree program—in accounting, not any of the liberal arts. I have never worked as a paid editor of either content or writing

1

mechanics.

So what makes me think I may be qualified to tell authors how they can polish their commercial fiction projects? First, I have sold over a hundred pieces of genre fiction including novels, novellas, and short stories to a variety of publishers from major New York houses to well-known e-book publishers. I have also self-published successfully. I have written and produced many short how-to articles on various writing topics, and presented them at conferences and other gatherings of writing professionals.

More important, I have a knack—some of my critique partners will say an unfortunate one—for spotting typos, punctuation errors, comma splices, misplaced modifiers, incorrectly used words, and so on. My English teachers in middle school and high school deserve the credit.

Fortunately or unfortunately, depending on the circumstances, I happen to have the innate mindset for retaining seemingly inconsequential facts when the occasion arises. That makes me a horrible content editor because I can't see through a forest of simple mechanical errors without a voice in my head screaming, every time I spot a misspelling, wrong tense, misplaced modifier or a malapropism (e.g., a misspoken or mistyped word that has a similar sound but a totally different meaning from the intended word).

That same trait makes me a really good copyeditor. I can tell whether someone's writing is technically correct, at least in the context of popular fiction, otherwise known somewhat derisively in literary circles as "genre fiction."

If an author is intent on selling his or her work, he or she can use the self-editing tips I've compiled in this book to improve the chances of that work being sold, whether to a publishing company or to end consumers via self-publishing. Readers' tolerance levels toward books riddled with mechanical errors will range between zero and moderate.

Self-editing for Writers is absolutely not a substitute for the second, third, or even fourth pair of critical eyes. Nobody's work is so flawless that rough drafts should be tossed into a professional editor's hand for a line edit—or God forbid, into a self-publishing template and on to an unsuspecting public.

By taking the preliminary step of self-editing genre fiction, a writer can vastly improve his or her chances for getting successfully published and becoming beloved by editors and readers alike.

Why Bother?

Why bother with self-editing? An author's best friends can be his editors, but every author will do himself or herself a favor by making his story as clean as it can be before passing it along to someone who may or may not see the storytelling gem that's hiding inside.

After all, most loyal friends/fans aren't likely to search through the work with an eye toward finding errors. The ones who are so inclined, as I am, will often miss inconsistencies in fact and character names that morph during the course of the story—because they are too focused on spotting and correcting

4

mechanical errors.

Acquiring editors all want to find that next great American novel, but the degree of patience they are willing to devote to finding a diamond in the rough can vary from saint-like to virtually zip-zero-zilch, depending on such capricious factors as the editor's current workload, social life or lack thereof, and so on.

Needless to say, an acquiring editor whose workload is heavy—and editors' workloads always are, at least according to them—is more likely to look kindly upon a manuscript that doesn't promise them many tedious hours, correcting errors in rudimentary spelling, grammar and punctuation.

You see, most editors can't see through a dense forest of errors and discover the masterpiece beneath it. It's the rare manuscript that survives a first editorial impression of, "Hey, this writer doesn't know the first thing about how to write." That writer's storytelling talent must show through clearly. If it doesn't pass that first look, the story will quickly find its way across the office to the reject pile. When that happens, the editor will sigh with relief that she didn't allow the brief glimpse of talent she saw in the first few pages to set herself up for a long ordeal of remedial tutoring. She may allow herself a moment's regret that the writer might become a wonderful storyteller if only he would master the writing craft.

So, you say that it doesn't matter if your manuscript has errors. Heck, you know that most readers won't catch them. So what if acquiring editors have turned down your masterpiece? You can still put that book up independently on Amazon and other online distributors, sit back and let the money start rolling in while you write your next book and/or promote the one that's out there on social media.

Oh, really? The previous paragraph is fiction—an understatement bordering on the delusional. True, most small errors won't jump out into the face of most readers. "Most," however, is not "all," and even the least picky reader will complain if he/she notices frequent mechanical errors in a self-published book. More to the point, the reader may be inclined to put down the book, but most likely he will remember your name and bad-mouth you to his interest groups.

This means lost income from previously willing buyers, which is always unacceptable in any business, but even more so in the production of "popular" products. People need fuel and shelter, regardless of the quality available to them—your product may *become* fuel if it gets cold enough. Your business is quite literally at the mercy of your readers, and every great author is mindful and respectful of this fact.

The most successful independently published authors self-edit their work before letting it out of their hands. A majority of them then pay a freelance editor, copyeditor and formatter to get it in shape to put up for sale.

Self-editing, as discussed in this book, is a search-and-correct mission through grammar, spelling and punctuation—functions that usually are handled in final form by publishing houses' copyeditors as opposed to their "line" or "content" editors who generally are the ones who acquire rights to works of fiction.

Readers of popular fiction range from the barely

literate, through average high school and college graduates, to multi-degreed professionals. Most of them, no matter their academic backgrounds, will choose genre fiction whose subject(s) interest them. This means they will be likely to know enough about the topic that they will spot obvious errors of fact, which is why it is a good idea to engage a private editor and/or beta readers who are knowledgeable in the genre and reasonably familiar with the time period and locale where the book is set. (The writer will, of course, have researched the material being presented as fact, before using it in his or her book.)

Self-editing focuses on the easy parts of storytelling. Gearing one's writing to the widest audience makes common sense. The more people who can easily understand the story you are telling, the more profitable your work becomes. Even so called "grammar Nazis" like myself and many editors, who pick off every mechanical error before angrily trashing the work, can and will forgive a story for being written at a lower reading level. So long as a great story is conveyed in an easily consumable way, you will take the readers where your imagination goes!

People like this tend to be obsessive about catching easy-to-spot errors in books for which they've paid their hard-earned money. They expect authors to write reasonably well in a technical sense while they're spinning interesting stories. They assume the authors have been as tortured in the middle grades as they were, because much of writing mechanics are presented and pounded into students' heads at that level.

Stated simply, no author will escape having a few readers who are grammar Nazis. Such readers will toss aside books at the sight of a second comma splice or run-on sentence. They will discard authors forever from their favorites lists if they mistake "their" or "they're" for "there." If they see too many words repeated too close together, they will shake their heads in disbelief—and relegate the book to the trash.

If that author is really unlucky, the disgusted reader will then dash off an email and complain to the bookseller (Amazon, Smashwords or other distributor where they bought the book) that the book fails to meet reasonable standards of readability/literacy. As fast as a magician's sleight of hand, the book gets taken down from the distributors' sites until the author fixes the mistakes. Money gets refunded to the complainant. Authors don't get royalties.

The disgusted reader may post unflattering reviews about the technical errors he or she spotted, which will undoubtedly cost the writer yet more sales. Not to mention embarrassment.

That said, I must admit I'm a Grammar Nazi of the worst order. I have gone so far as to suggest that my critique partners print the various tenses of the verbs, "Lie" and "Lay", and paste them onto their computer monitors so as not to keep confusing them. This, of course, is far from the worst mistake a writer can make.

I must admit that a majority of readers probably wouldn't even notice when a writer mistakes the meanings and tenses of those two simple words. I've seen them overlooked in novels that came from the most respected major publishers. I guess I can thank my teachers for having drilled those particular rules into my head!

Disclaimer: Because of my eclectic background, I can tell you whether your writing is technically correct. I probably can't tell you in didactic terms exactly why it is wrong. Never having taught creative writing, I haven't found a valid reason to keep grammar rules themselves on the tip of my tongue.

I can, however, spot errors a mile away. While I don't necessarily know exactly what rule has been broken, I know when something's wrong. The same is true of a lot of potential readers of genre fiction, and seeing obvious errors disrupts their enjoyment of the book.

Having good writing technique doesn't make a fiction writer "good." The talent to tell stories is paramount. Storytelling ability is inborn, but it can be honed with practice and careful attention to sensual details— sight, sound, taste, smell, touch, and feel. Writing technique, on the other hand, is learned. Admittedly, learning that lesson requires more effort from some authors than from others, usually in direct proportion to the meanness of their primary and middle school instructors.

There is no excuse for any author turning in a book—whether to the biggest New York publishing company or to a self-publisher for immediate publication—if it's spattered with errors in spelling, grammar, punctuation or syntax.

An aspiring author has all the tools he or she needs, between critique partners/beta readers, up-to-the-minute writing software—and this little book, which will give some tips about the craft of writing that often get swept to the wayside beneath every author's desire to show and tell an unforgettable story.

Self-editing doesn't have to take forever. It doesn't require weeks of tedious examination of each and every word. In the coming sections of this book, I'll share some simple tricks that can do wonders toward polishing a story—making it shine in the eyes of people whose job it is to determine whether it lives or dies, figuratively speaking of course.

There are three main elements to editing. Many publishing houses split the editing function between the "line editor", who reads the manuscript and makes changes he or she deems necessary to make the book he has contracted fit into the notch or line for which it was contracted, and the copyeditor who is charged with correcting misspellings, grammatical errors and obvious errors of fact.

With most publishers, a line editor is the person who accepts a book proposal. It will then be "line edited," but not necessarily by the editor who accepted it. The copyeditor gets the book only after the line editor has signed off on for content, house style, and so on. *Self-editing cannot replace a conscientious professional edit, but it can make your book more likely to be accepted by a publishing company. If you are paying a freelance editor, your cost will doubtless be less if the material you give the freelancer is a mechanically clean manuscript.*

This book focuses on the sorts of sloppy writing that will get a book rejected even though there is promise of great storytelling in the proposal—the kinds of errors that can easily be fixed using the self-editing suggestions within, things that have the potential of turning a rejected storytelling masterpiece into a *New*

York Times bestseller.

Section II

Using Software Tools to Help You Self-edit

This section deals with simple errors that modern software can sometimes help to correct. It also presents situations in which these tools can't always take care of authors' mistakes. It has been divided into the most common tools that can be helpful to authors.

The writing modules included in Microsoft Office, Corel WordPerfect, Open Office, Scrivener and other software packages are things of wonder. I doubt that we could function efficiently without them. (Because I use Microsoft Office and am most familiar with its current iterations, I will use "Word" as a generic term to mean any modern word processing software. For the most part, all of popular word-processing software modules have similar capabilities.)

Disclaimer: This book is not a manual on how to set

Word up or format it for writing your book. I am not an expert on the various versions of Word that still are in use by writers, I haven't used WordPerfect since 2004—and I've never utilized Open Office or any other writing software that's out there in cyberspace. I often have to search Microsoft's tutorials to find how to use the Word features that I may need. Publishers generally have templates for formatting manuscripts—and many of them also have developed tutorials that show exactly how to use common functions in everything from Word 2000 on to the most current, cloud-based Word 365. (If publishers of fiction show a preference for one vendor's software, it is always for Microsoft Office. At least that has been my experience over the past nearly twenty years of working with publishers.)

Find/Search/Replace Tools

When you see blue lines below text in Word documents, Word is trying to tell you that there's a problem with grammar, punctuation or syntax. You will need to look carefully, not only at the text that's blue-lined but also at nearby text, discover what's wrong, and fix the problem manually. Blue-lined items can be as minor as having two periods at the end of a sentence, or as mind-boggling as having Word indicate you've made a boo-boo that you scratch your head trying to identify when you first look at it.

Common errors that show up blue-lined have to do with missing or duplicated punctuation marks, commas instead of periods at the end of sentences and extra spaces, particularly at the beginnings and endings of paragraphs. These can be difficult to spot on re-examination, so the easiest thing to do is follow the tip and perform a find/replace until there are no more to replace.

Tip: Before addressing individual blue-lined items in Word, you can save time by doing several iterations of Find/Replace—[find ..X/replace with Y. Find two dashes, replace with em-dash symbol. Find two spaces, replace with one space. Find three periods, replace with ellipsis symbol—and so on.

Tip: After you have finished making content changes, immediately before submitting your book to a publisher (or publishing it yourself), repeat these find/replace actions. It's amazing how those tiny errors can crop back up after you have made changes to your first draft.

Tip: Watch carefully for blue-line items that show up after you have made content changes. Often, when wording has been changed, you end up with subject and verb tenses not matching when they matched in the original text.

Spell Checkers

Spell-checkers can become writers' best friends, if—and that's a big "if"—the writer has a good grasp of exactly which of two or more correct, similar sounding words he or she needs to use in a particular situation. Unfortunately, spell-checkers cannot determine whether a correctly spelled word is the particular word a writer intended to use.

Word can be set up to autocorrect misspellings (combinations of letters that are not in its built-in dictionary). Alternately, it can mark them in red for the author to correct in a subsequent self-edit.

I do not use the auto-correct function in Word. Why? Because of fortunate genes and great teachers, I am an instinctively good speller. I am also the sort of typist who immediately senses typos and corrects them on the fly, which is why I was an abysmally poor typist on a typewriter but am pretty fast and accurate on a computer keyboard. I don't use autocorrect because my manuscripts don't have a lot of red-lined words that need to be fixed as a part of my self-editing process, and because using auto-correct would most likely produce more problems for me to fix than it would prevent.

Some writers may want to use auto-correct if they are either poor typists and/or poor spellers. It's an option that can work, but only if the writer is careful to examine his/her text in context and manually fix correctly spelled words that are *not* the words that he/she intended to use.

Tip: Even good spellers have words that are their figurative Waterloos. Mine is "ecstasy," which can be problematic since I write mostly sensual/erotic romances where that word tends to crop up every now and then. I have that word, and a few others, on a checklist that I pull out when self-editing my manuscripts, using Word's FIND/REPLACE option, using "FIND" to locate the misspellings I most frequently commit—ecstacy, extasy, and so on—and "REPLACE" them with the correctly spelled ecstasy.

If seeing a character's unusually spelled name, a foreign-language word or a correct word that doesn't happen to be in Word's extensive built-in dictionary annoys you as a writer, you may add the word to the software's dictionary. If you do, Word will no longer recognize that sometimes frequently used name as being misspelled and cease its decoration of your pages with repeated red lines.

Tip: I do not recommend adding misspelled words that you may use occasionally with the intent of adding color to dialogue, to Word's dictionary. If you do, your manuscript may end up with a lot of manufactured contractions that you did not intend to use.

Tip: You may want to keep a list of redlined words that you have added to Word's dictionary, and delete them after your manuscript/series has been put to bed—this can keep you from inadvertently having a name/slang word applicable only to a particular book or series pop up in a subsequent project.

Tip: If you use dictation software for whatever

reason, you will find words that **Dragon Naturally Speaking** or other voice-recognition software often misunderstands as you talk to it. This is not the software's fault, but rather that it doesn't understand the nuances of your speech patterns or accent. "Their," "They're" and "There" aren't pronounced exactly the same, but they're close. If you're typing, you will probably know which word you're using and spell it correctly in context. The software may not be able to discern subtle differences like this, which means that you will want to add the ones it commonly interprets incorrectly to your list of correctly spelled but possibly incorrect words to add to your self-edit list.

Tip: Generally speaking, the latest versions of voice recognition software that are compatible with your word processing software are most accurate at recognizing your speech.

Using AutoCorrect Functions

Auto-formatting in Word allows an author to create ellipses, em-dashes and other symbols easily, by typing familiar symbols and allowing the software to convert it to the desired symbol. It also provides an option to create "curly" instead of "straight" quotes, which most publishers use as "house style."

Tip: In Appendix A, I have listed the most common AutoCorrect settings that I turn on in my own rough drafts. You may find the list helpful, keeping in mind that you need to consider your own publishers' house style(s) in setting these options.

The find/replace function I referred to in more detail at the beginning of this section can make life much easier by ferreting out common errors in mechanics, consistency and punctuation. It can also help you to find and correct words that you tend to use or type incorrectly.

Tip: In Appendix B, I have included examples of words that can be transposed while typing or misunderstood while dictated by my personal voice recognition software. It is by no means intended to be all-encompassing, but simply a series of illustrations of a few gaffes I have made and had to correct from time to time.

Word's built-in helpers are almost unending. I am not an expert on most of the features, as I use the software almost exclusively to write and edit manuscripts.

In my limited experience, the best tutor on using software's auto-formatting function globally is its manufacturer's website. Microsoft, for example, has excellent tutors on setting up and utilizing the capabilities a writer needs to produce the cleanest manuscripts.

Remember, Machines Can't Substitute for Human Eyes

There are many things an author's software can do for him/her toward self-editing rough drafts.

Word or the writing software of your choice can help you ensure that your manuscript's fonts, paragraph setup, indentation and general formatting are uniform. If set up properly, it can see that all of your quotes are curly—or straight, as you choose—and that none of your ellipses appear as three periods instead of the proper symbols.

While you can use your software to help you avoid mistakes in spelling, punctuation and grammar, that very intelligent but robotic machine cannot substitute for eyes-on scrutiny by a human being—preferably by you, before you hand it off to a professional editor or reader who will most likely be much less understanding of you for using a word found in Word's extensive dictionary that was not the one you intended.

Section III

The Ten (or More) Commandments about Punctuation

Learn and heed Ann's commandments for punctuating commercial fiction. The general rule in informal writing is that less is better—but with exceptions—as there are to nearly every rule.

1. Thou shalt not use semicolons.

Semicolons can connect two independent clauses or serve as "super-commas" in long, complex sentences with multiple lists or dependent clauses. They are correct and frequently used in legal briefs and scholarly treatises—but not in informal fiction. So say most editors.

Tip: In informal writing, if you think you need a

semicolon, you most likely need two sentences—or an em dash. You don't need that semicolon in 999 cases out of a thousand.

Example: With just four color cartridges, you can print thousands of colors; you. You will use the black one most often as a writer.

2. Thou shalt not use colons.

Colons precede lists—in formal writing. In informal writing such as commercial fiction, lists are preceded by an em-dash and separated by commas—when they are used at all.

Example: Color printers have only four cartridges—black, magenta, yellow and cyan.

3. Thou shalt use exclamation marks sparingly, if at all.

Tip: Let the dialogue itself convey the sense of excitement or urgency.

4. Thou shalt not use unnecessary dialogue tags.

Use dialogue tags only when needed in order to ensure that the reader will be clear as to who is speaking.

Tip: All dialogue tags' action must be synonymous with "said"—i.e., he said, she replied, etc.

Tip: Tagged dialogue is begun with a comma, question mark or (rarely) an exclamation point at the end of dialogue. The tag is punctuated with a period.

Example: "I believe that John has the book," said Mary.

5. Thou shalt not confuse dialogue tags with directionals.

Directionals, separate sentences that identify the speaker, are often confused with tags (see above). In many cases it is preferable to substitute a directional for a dialogue tag, especially when there are many participants in a conversation and it isn't readily clear who is the one speaking.

Tip: A directional is a complete sentence, immediately following direct speech. It can convey action, whereas a dialogue tag only conveys the identity of the speaker.

Example: "I believe that John has the book." Mary turned to John. "Didn't I give it to you?"

Tip: In the example above, it is obvious that Mary is still speaking because when a new speaker says something, a new paragraph is begun.

Tip: When using a directional, end the direct quote with a period or question mark, as appropriate, and the close quote character. It is easy to confuse the punctuation of these two speaker identifiers.

6. Thou shalt not leave quotes open.

Double quotes—"curly" ones—surround dialogue. (If writing for a UK publisher, single quote symbols, the same as apostrophes on keyboard, are used to surround dialogue.) In the United States, single quotes are used only within double quotes, or to refer to the proper name of a work of art, music or literature. Italicizing such titles is often preferable, however, to single quotation marks.

Example: "I am reading 'The Highwayman' to my nephew."

7. Thou shalt not use multiple punctuation marks for single sentences.

Whether accidentally (..) or on purpose (!?!), no single sentence can have more than one terminating punctuation mark.

Accidents happen. Double periods may easily be found and destroyed by using the search-replace capabilities of your word processing software.(So can double question marks and exclamation points for that matter, if you tend to try to double punctuate sentences with those marks.)

While using multiple punctuation marks purposely

may seem handy to convey shock/disbelief/anger or other emotions, the point of view character's feelings about what's going on may be better revealed through word choice.

8. Thou shalt use or not use Oxford commas consistently.

You may use the Oxford comma, by which the last item in a series of like objects is set off with a comma as well as "and", "or", "nor", or similar conjunctions—or you may choose to let the conjunction stand in place of that comma. Keep in mind that some publishers specify one or the other, but if the choice is yours, either is correct in informal writing.

Tip: be careful about leaving out the Oxford comma in complex series of phrases/clauses. Sometimes doing so makes the sentence difficult to parse.

Example of Oxford comma use: *Mary, Tom, and Jerry went to school.*

Example of eschewing Oxford comma: *Mary, Tom and Jerry went to school.*

Once you choose, be consistent.

9. Thou shalt not mix conventions of punctuation in the same book.

It is common in commercial fiction to see what is generally referred to as "open punctuation," a growing group of broken formal writing rules that have become acceptable in genre fiction. If you choose to use open punctuation, use it consistently throughout the book.

Example: "Me too", which your high school English teacher said must have a comma preceding the "too", but which is often seen as I just wrote it, is okay so long as you minimize use of commas wherever doing so doesn't impair reader's enjoyment of the book.

10. Thou shalt not inundate thy text with italics.

Italics are more difficult to read than straight text. In general, use them only to denote a foreign word not generally used in English, or to set apart the title of a book in text.

Short flashbacks—no more than a sentence or two— may also be placed in italics. If you can't avoid using a long flashback to convey backstory information, don't use italics. Instead, indent the flashback about a half-inch from left and right margins and use regular text—but try hard not to utilize long flashbacks. They're difficult to do well, and they tend to distract readers from present action.

Tip: A little off-topic, but it's not a good idea to confuse readers by dropping bits of text or dialogue in foreign languages, italicized or not, if most won't get the meaning without explanation. "Si senor" or "buenas noches" are okay—almost everybody will be able to figure those out. Like spices in food, a little continental color can go a long way.

11. **Thou shalt not forget how to punctuate possessives or plural proper names.**

Proper names, other than those ending in "S," are made possessive by adding " **'s**."

Proper names ending in "S" can be made possessive by adding an " **'** ", or an " **'s**," but be consistent!

Plural proper names, not possessive, are made plural by adding "**s**" or "**es**" as appropriate—no possessive symbol.

Examples: Jane (singular) Jane's (singular possessive) Janes (plural)

Jane is going to a convention of Janes. Jane's brother is going too.

Jones (singular) Jones' (singular possessive) Joneses (plural) Joneses' (plural possessive)

Jones is a common family name. Jones' book is old. They are all Joneses.

Tip: Make life easy on yourself. Do not give major

characters either first or last names ending in "s."

12. Thou shalt not write sentences, correctly punctuated or not, that are difficult for readers to parse.

There's nothing that frustrates a reader much more than having to read a sentence repeatedly in order to understand it.

Tip: If a sentence takes up more than two and a half typed lines of normal-size print, chances are it has a comma splice or is actually more than one sentence run onto another. If, upon close examination, you find that your sentence is technically correct and is still so long, chances are it would be easier to parse if you split it into two complete sentences.

Tip: If you need to diagram a sentence to determine whether or not it is correct, you most likely need to simplify.

Tip: If you feel an overwhelming urge to use a

semicolon in a sentence, chances are that you need to make that sentence into two or more sentences.

13.Thou shalt not misplace modifiers or use improper antecedents.

"While chewing on a bone, Mary petted her dog." While readers can get a laugh out of reading these common mistakes, they will most likely lose track of the story line while chuckling.

Tip: Re-check sentences that have initial dependent clauses, because this is where most people seem to misplace their modifiers. (Misplaced modifiers can also occur when modifiers that are supposed to apply to the subject of a sentence look as though they apply to a terminal clause.)

Less humorous, yet more common, are cases where authors use improper antecedents, or an ambiguous or erroneous noun that precedes a pronoun. This isn't as likely in scenes where there are only two characters of the opposite sex, but it occasionally happens even

37

in such a scene when one of the characters is speaking about a character not present in the scene.

Tip: There are many places on the web where an author who isn't clear about rules such as antecedents can find expert guidance. A simple rule of thumb on antecedents is to look back as you write and be certain that the character you're referring to by a pronoun is the same one to whom you most recently referred by name.

Tip: Be careful not to over-use character names when "he" or "she" will adequately identify the speaker or thinker. This is especially important in scenes with one man and one woman. Once you've identified who they are, you may freely continue the scene without using proper names again, as long as there's no likelihood a reader will confuse who is talking or thinking. You will find that in scenes with multiple active characters and/or scenes with two people of the same gender, you will need to insert proper names more frequently.

Section IV

Finding and Fixing Word Choice Errors

For the most part, spelling errors can be found with the help of your software's spell-check function which will either AutoCorrect or red-line misspelled words, depending on how Word has been AutoFormatted.

Sometimes, though, words come up that tend to stymie the system, not to mention your speech to text software. Spelling gaffes have several faces, beginning with the ones that are least noticeable and objectionable to most readers—and progressing to those that tear out grammar-Nazis' hair when they spot egregious spelling errors in published books.

Correctly spelled words that give you choices

Example: Is it "Goodbye" or "good-bye"? Either is correct, but please use one or the other consistently.

Most common in this category are words that are variant spellings in American English and preferred spellings in British English. Generally, for an American audience, an author would choose the American standard: *armor* instead of *armour*, *behavior* instead of *behaviour*, *realize* instead of *realise*, *whiskey* instead of *whisky*, etc.

More examples include *ax* v. *axe*, doughnut v. donut, and too many more to enumerate here.

Tip: When in doubt, employ your computer and do an internet search for "preferred spelling of _____ American English or British English," (if writing for UK audience).

Coined or made up spelling of regional dialects—to be used only sparingly if you want readers to stay engaged

Occasional dropping of the terminal or initial letter of

a word and replacing it with an apostrophe (a single quotation mark), can indicate to readers that a character is a southerner, an Irishman, or of some other ethnicity/educational level known for these speech patterns. It can add characterization and lend color to dialogue.

Intentionally misspelled words, such as a character dropping the "ey" from "honey" if she's a southerner or writing "dogie" instead of "doggie" if the speaker's a cowboy talking about his cattle, can aid in characterization without causing your readers headaches. You have to take care, though, not to create text that, while colorful, is apt to slow reading down so much that readers will discard the book.

A rule of thumb for me is that if the dialect slows my reading, it's too much. I want enough color to get the point that the reader is a cowboy, a Scots Highlander, an Irishman or an American southerner—but not so much that I feel the author is trying to hit me over the head with overkill.

In general, I suggest limiting dialect to spoken dialogue—although it may occasionally work in

41

internal dialogue, also known as indirect thought.

Tip: Pick one word—maybe as many as two or three but not a lot more—that the character always says in dialect, and write the rest of his/her dialogue in standard English.

Tip: When you are AutoFormatting, if you set Word to do curly quotes, set them both for single as well as double quotes. That way, when the single one is an apostrophe, it will show up correctly whether you've used it to replace the beginning or the end of the word you're shortening.

Wrong words—sudden death on readers

Homonyms (words that sound alike but have different meanings and are spelled differently) play havoc, especially but not always in dictated manuscripts. They also crop up when the author is typing and manages to type a real word but not the word he or she meant.

Whether the dictating software misunderstood or you

don't have a clear picture as to which similar sounding word is appropriate in the context you're using doesn't matter.

There's little that will turn a reader off faster than spotting mistakes like this. *There*, *their* and *they're*, collectively, are among the worst culprits for being interchanged. *There* means "in that place." *Their* is possessive: "belonging to them"—and the least often misused one, *they're*, is a contraction of "they are."

The verbs *lie* and *lay*, are regularly misused when the author means "recline" or "place." The easiest way to distinguish the words is to memorize the fact that *lie* cannot have a direct object while *lay* must have one.

Example: A person *lies* on a bed, while someone *lays* an object onto the bed. (The past tense of these verbs works in the same way, grammatically speaking. This is where the confusion gets worse. The tense forms of *lie* are *lie*, *lay* and *lain*. *Lay's* tense forms are *lay*, *laid* and laid.)

Other examples of words which occasionally get mistaken for one another, especially by dictation software, could take up an entire dictionary. I have compiled Appendix B which contains words I've seen mistaken for other valid words, either published books or my own rough drafts when I dictated them instead of typing. The lists are by no means complete. The best way to avoid turning in books with gaffes like these is to read carefully and make manual corrections.

Tip: If you know you tend to make the same typos/word choice errors frequently, start at the beginning of the book with the "Find" function and look at every instance of the word you habitually mistype or that your dictation software misinterprets. Replace them if they're incorrect in context.

Right Words, Wrong Choice

To convey meaning and keep your reader on point, your most powerful tool can be word choice.

Many words are synonyms (different words with the same or similar meanings). That doesn't mean that all synonyms are interchangeable.

Tip: Don't use general words when more specific ones will paint a better word picture.

Tip: In general, avoid using synonyms that are so obscure that most readers will have to do a Google search in order to find out exactly what the word means. (Remember, genre fiction is written to a maximum fifth grade literacy level.)

Example: (general) Mary got out of the car and hit her head.

(better)   Mary fell out of the car and hit her head.

Mary jumped out of the car and hit her head.

45

A thesaurus provides a wide choice of synonyms for simple words. Beware that not all synonyms' full meaning will be what you intended for your character to do or say.

Example:

Tip: If you are putting in a very unusual word as a synonym for a more common one, be very sure that you know the nuances and subtleties of that ten dollar word's meaning. (If you pluck out a synonym at random from a list of synonyms, you may be sorry. Some readers are bound to get a good laugh that you don't realize that your word doesn't fit within the context of the character's action.

You want to limit repetition of words in the same sentence, the same paragraph, the same page or scene. I have found that the length of the word has an inverse relationship with the likelihood that an editor or reader will notice two or more occurrences of the word in close proximity.

Example: No one will comment on the frequent reiteration of articles and pronouns, particularly short ones. They will note repetition of longer words, particularly descriptive adjectives and verbs.

Tip: You want to vary your choice of words. On the same page, a character or characters may say or refer in thought to the same general action several times, but you should try to replace duplicate words close enough together to notice them with appropriate synonyms.

In the interest of not distracting or annoying readers, do not repeat the same significant words too often, particularly within easy readers' view.

Example: Tom rode his horse along the fence, keeping an eye out for the horse that had gone missing last night. So far he hadn't spotted her, but he saw a break in the fence and a horse's hoof prints in the sandy field. (Terrible writing, but technically correct)

Tom rode his stallion alongside the fence, keeping an eye out for the chestnut mare that had gone missing last night. So far he hadn't spotted her, but he did notice a break in the fence and hoof prints in the sandy field. (Better, still not great)

47

A Word or Two about Pronouns

Yes, personal pronouns are words that can be substituted for character names. When they are correctly used, they can make for smoother reading and keep the author from having to repeat a character's actual name.

Problems occur when personal pronouns are substituted for the names without a clear antecedent that identifies the character.

Examples: Mary called Joan. (Correct)

She (Joan) called Tom. (Correct if Joan is the last proper name referred to before the pronoun)

There's nothing that frustrates a reader much more than having to read a sentence repeatedly in order to understand it.

Tip: There are many places on the web where an author who isn't clear about rules such as antecedents can find expert guidance. A simple rule of thumb on antecedents is to look back as you write and be certain that the character you're referring to by a pronoun is the same one to whom you most recently referred by name.

Tip: Be careful not to over-use character names when "he" or "she" will adequately identify the speaker or thinker. This is especially important in scenes with one man and one woman. Once you've identified who they are, you may freely continue the scene without using proper names again, as long as there's no likelihood a reader will confuse who is talking or thinking. You will find that in scenes with multiple active characters and/or scenes with two people of the same gender, you will need to insert proper names more frequently.

Be sure when using personal pronouns, which you should as long as they convey the proper message, that you're saying what you intended to say. there's nothing that frustrates a reader much more than having to read a sentence repeatedly in order to understand who is speaking about whom or what.

Beware of unnecessarily long and complex sentences.

Chances are, if a sentence takes up more than two and a half typed lines of normal-size print, that it has a comma splice or is actually more than one sentence run onto another. If, upon close examination, you find that your sentence is technically correct, you still might consider splitting it into two complete sentences.

Tip: It is often said that commercial fiction should be written at an approximate fifth grade level of literacy.

Tip: If you need to diagram a sentence to determine whether or not it is correct, you most likely need to simplify.

Tip: If you feel an overwhelming urge to use a semicolon in a sentence, chances are that you need to make that sentence into two or more sentences.

Search out and destroy misplaced modifiers.

Misplaced modifiers occur most often when a writer

has re-worded a sentence, often with the intention of varying sentence structure to make for more interesting reading.

Example: The original sentence was this—*Mary petted her dog while it was chewing on a bone.*

You re-wrote it so the sentence structure wouldn't be just another subject, verb, object—*While chewing on a bone, Mary petted her dog.*

While readers can get a laugh out of reading this second sentence, they will most likely lose track of the story line while chuckling.

Tip: Re-check sentences that have initial dependent clauses, because this is where most people seem to misplace their modifiers. (Misplaced modifiers can also occur when modifiers that are supposed to apply to the subject of a sentence look as though they apply to a terminal clause.)

Less humorous but more common are cases where authors use improper antecedents, or an ambiguous or erroneous noun that precedes a pronoun. This isn't as

51

likely in scenes where there only two characters of the opposite sex, but it occasionally happens even in such a scene when one of the characters is speaking about a character who is not present in the scene.

Tip: If you need to diagram a sentence to determine whether or not it is correct, you most likely need to simplify.

Tip: If you feel an overwhelming urge to use a semicolon in a sentence, chances are that you need to make that sentence into two or more sentences.

Beware of Character Names that Evolve

This shouldn't need saying, but having done it myself, I want to remind you to check your characters' names, and make sure that Mary is Mary throughout the book and didn't somehow evolve into "Mari," "Marie," or something entirely different.

(This isn't to say that one character can't be called his complete name by his parents and a nickname by his significant other, or vice versa.)

52

Section V

Taking Person and Tense Agreement Seriously

Genre fiction is usually written in third person, simple past tense, although first person, simple past tense is frequently employed in mysteries and detective thrillers.

Errors occur between person and tense most frequently after an author has re-worded a sentence and failed to change the tense of the verb to match a new/modified subject. They also happen when a writer is using (or has changed) a new verb but failed to modify the verb form when the new verb has irregular conjugation.

Books abound on grammar rules and handling the match of verb forms to various subjects. In this section, I will mention a few of the errors I've most often encountered when reading genre fiction.

Tenses of regularly conjugated verbs in English

The past and "perfect" tenses of most regularly conjugated verbs in English consist of the word + the suffix "ed." (*pass, fail, enter, fill, climb, die, stay,* and so on)

Unfortunately, there are many commonly used verbs that are irregular, starting with ones that consist of only two or three letters. The most common ones that come to mind are conjugated below.

"be"

I am, you are, he/she/it is

I was, you were, he/she/it was

I have been, you have been, he/she/it had been

I had been, you had been, he/she/it had been

We are, you are, they are

We were, you were, they were

We have been, you have been, they have been

Substitute single proper name for "he/she/it," plural one for "they"

"go"

I go, you go, he/she/it goes

I went, you went, he/she/it went

I have gone, you have gone, he/she/it has gone

We go, you go, he/she/it goes

We went, you went, they went

We have gone, you have gone, they have gone

"do"

I do, you do, he/she/it does

I did, you did, he/she/it did

I have done, you have done, he/she/it has done

We do, you do, he/she/it does

We did, you did, they did

We have done, you have done, they have done

"pay," "lay,"

As with many other words ending in "y," the past and perfect tenses drop the "y" and substitute "id."

"lie"

When the meaning of "lie" is "to recline," the present, past and perfect tenses of it are "lie, lay, lain"

When "lie" means "to tell an untruth," its conjugation is "lie, lied, lied"

These are just a few examples of person/tense variations of form depending on subject and tense. Change one and you will need to follow through, not only with these common, small verbs but also with others.

When in doubt, turn to internet search and be certain you're right, considering the context in which a verb is used as well as the meaning of it that you intend to convey.

Past tense or Past Perfect?

Without going into depth, simple past tense is generally used to convey present action in most genre novels.

Present perfect tense (has gone) indicates that the

action is ongoing.

Past perfect tense (had gone) lets the reader know the action was in the distant past when that isn't stated specifically in context.

Example: Henry *liked* his new toy as well as he *had liked* the one he *broke* last month. (Here, because it is stated how long ago the toy was broken, the past perfect would not be necessary in that clause.)

Section VI

A Few Words about Point of View

Point of view (POV) refers to the character from whose mind/brain/point of view you are telling your story. There are entire books written on the subject, so I won't trouble you with a lengthy discussion of which POV you should use in your novel.

Briefly, all books written in first person ("I") convey the narrator's thoughts (your thoughts, actually) through the eyes of a single character—or of the narrator.

First person POV can be distant, a story told from a vantage point, conveying action but only the emotion that can be shown by the actors on the screen of the author's mind.

It can also be "close" first person, in which the story is told by a significant character (usually the hero in mysteries/thrillers, the heroine in Gothic romances). That character's emotions are revealed, while other characters' feelings come through only in what they do and say.

I have encountered a few close first-person books in which the narrator shifts from one chapter to another, with chapter headers that indicate who is seeing the whole picture in the chapter.

I have never seen a novel or novella written in second person ("you") POV.

Third person POV gives a writer the most flexibility in showing rather than telling a story, revealing the feelings of multiple characters. By limiting POV "cameras" to no more than two or three main characters and being careful to make clear when there is a change of "lens" from one character to the other, a writer can convey depth of emotion and maximum sensuality without confusing the reader.

Most romance-genre books and many women's fiction novels are written in third person, simple past tense, with limited POV characters. Usually both hero and heroine's POVs are shown. Occasionally a third character's POV will also insist on being heard.

Tip: The most mind-boggling rule that I had to digest before being able to write a cohesive, marketable romance was the concept of third-person, limited point of view. POV is a subject many authors ignore while others treat POV consistency as though it's the Holy Grail. What you choose to do is up to you, but you need to understand POV before you dare to ignore it.

Tip: a point of view character can only react to what he can observe. If he is not looking into a mirror, he cannot describe the details of what he is wearing— not to mention that doing so makes him seem to be a narcissist of the worst order.

Tip: The POV character cannot know what he/she can't observe. She can admire another character's appearance, wish he would comb his hair, notice tear stains on his cheeks—but she cannot know what anyone else is thinking, although she can form opinions based on what she observes in another character.

In self-editing, the only way I know to seek out bad POV is by carefully re-reading my scenes and determining whether a reader will be able to tell at first glance where my POV character has changed, and whether or not that change is so abrupt as to confuse or annoy if you've suddenly and jarringly switched from one character's POV to another.

Section VII

Summing it Up

Editing a book is a multifaceted process that involves checking of facts, modification of a writer's voice or tone so the book will fit within a stated publisher's line, and finally verifying the technical/mechanical correctness of the words themselves.

As for the facts presented, a writer's fact-checking processes should always precede commencement of writing. In order to write a credible story, the author has to know, in varying degrees of depth, about his or her characters—where did they grow up, how much schooling did each have, what they regularly do to perform their jobs, and so on.

Research of time and setting is critical, particularly if the time during which the book will be set is other than contemporary to the author. If, for instance, the story will be set in medieval England, the author will need to familiarize himself/herself with the mores of the period and place. If, on the other hand, the story will take place in a futuristic setting, the author will need to create a story world—and however improbable it may be, the rules of that made-up world must be consistently followed.

The author may seek out beta readers or a paid professional editor to perform the types of edits detailed above. They generally fall to the line editor—the person who reads for content and points out illogical story progression, inconsistent voice, and so on.

I'm unsure that an author can efficiently substitute for a line editor's contributions. I know, however, that self-editing for mechanical and technical errors will make a line editor's job far easier—and cheaper for the author who chooses to pay for that editor's time.

The wise writer will follow the tips in this book and make it as clean as it can be, before putting it into the hands of line editors. Editors who acquire books for publishers will not stay long with a poorly edited or unedited story, no matter how intriguing they may find the author's concept.

Paid freelance editors ("book doctors") can be engaged to perform the full edit functions for an author. Some charge by the page, others by the hour, with rates varying based on a writing sample the author sends in. That rate is going to much higher—exponentially higher in some cases—if the author's writing is riddled with mechanical/technical errors that he or she should have caught and fixed before letting another living soul look at his or her work.

Even major publishing companies split out the nitty-gritty mechanical edits of a book and assign a copyeditor, usually a freelance person, to do a final run-through of the line-edited book and fix any mechanical errors that have slipped through earlier.

Self-editing encompasses cleaning up the craft of writing, and just as a carpenter is expected to know how to use a hammer and nails, a writer is expected to hone his craft.

Self-editing should be the writer's first step in making his or her book as clean mechanically as it can be.

No beta reader, acquiring editor who may contract your book, or even a close friend or family member is likely to look hard enough to find a wonderful story if it's buried under a ton of obvious misspellings, bad grammar, and misused words. For that reason if no other, you should clean up the things you can easily do, using the tips in this book.

If you are a great storyteller who is completely clueless about how to write, your readers will never know it, because they'll toss the book after becoming fed up with the first few pages.

If a writer presents a wonderful story in a way that shows that he or she has mastered the craft of writing genre fiction, he or she will be on the road to success, and his or her readers will be enriched much more fully by the experiences the author has shared with them.

Appendix A

Autoformatting Word Processing Software

Microsoft Office 2013 or 365--Word

Microsoft Office's video tutorials/courses, accessed via its help feature, are invaluable in explaining the substantial changes from previous versions of Word. *I noticed but haven't tried **AutoCorrect In Context**, which theoretically could keep a person who can't distinguish among two correct words (there, their, they're—rite, right—indicated, indicted) on the right track by turning on that feature, which takes more computer memory than the base requirement for Office.*

http://support.office.microsoft.com/client/Choose-how-spell-check-and-grammar-check-work-71fd027a-be9c-42b0-8055-75f46324a16a?ui=en-US&rs=en-US&ad=US&NS=WINWORD&Version=15

Microsoft Office 2010--Word

https://support.office.com/en-us/article/Check-spelling-and-grammar-5cdeced7-d81d-47de-9096-efd0ee909227?ui=en-US&rs=en-US&ad=US

Microsoft Office 2007

https://support.office.com/en-au/article/Choose-how-spelling-and-grammar-checking-work-020ea19b-5fd3-4be7-9f01-723f0dc7b941

Microsoft Office 2003

Microsoft has discontinued support for Word 2003. Instructions to set writers' most commonly used options found in the software follow, with screen prints and explanations of how to use them. **Click on the main tab, Tools. Click on AutoCorrect Options.** This will take you to a screen with five tabs.. Writers generally need only concern themselves with these three tabs:

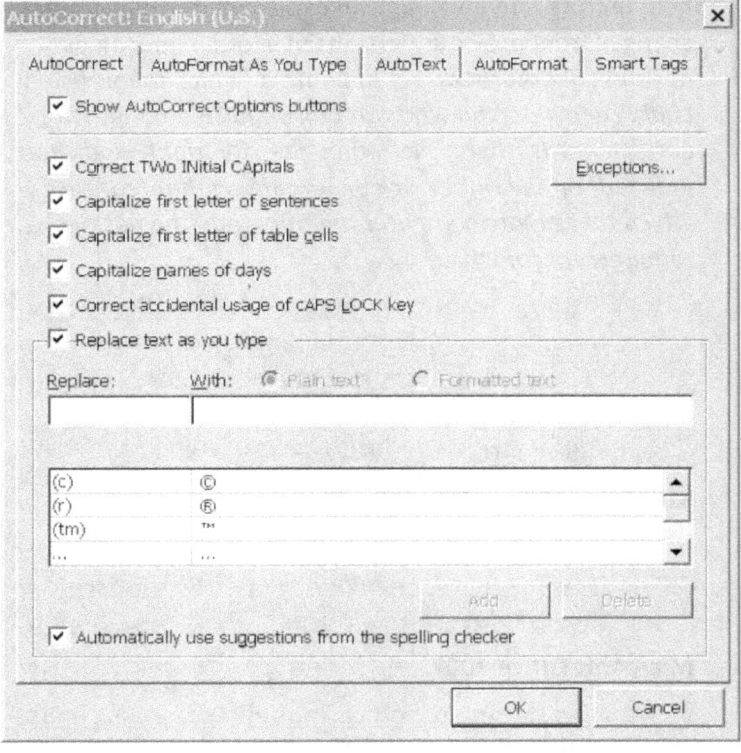

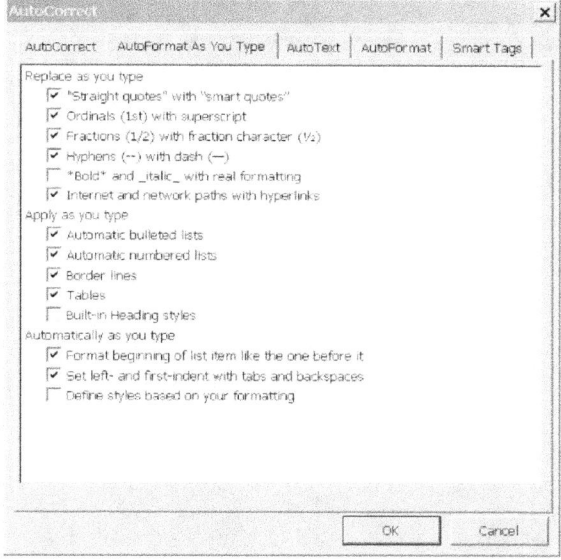

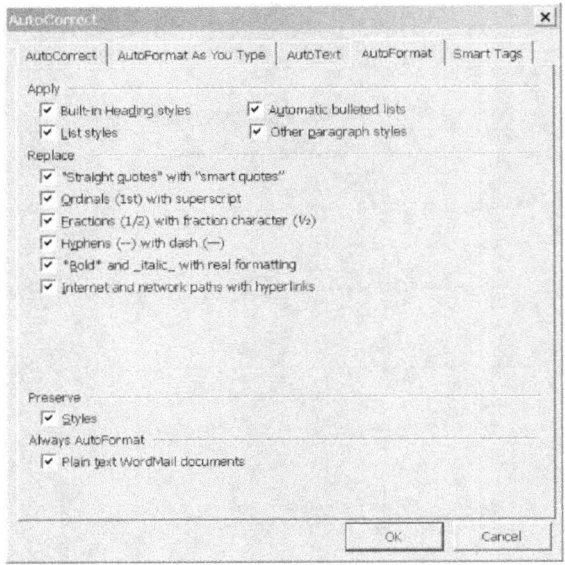

The autocorrect tab is useful to change double hyphens (--) to em dashes, "straight" quotes to "curly" ones, and three consecutive periods to ellipses. They are sometimes useful for telling Word to automatically correct typos resulting from transpositions that a writer realizes he or she habitually makes.

AutoFormat As You Type tab is used in combination with "AutoFormat" to tell the system to convert the symbols you usually type (three periods when you mean an ellipsis, or two hyphens when you mean an em-dash) but which aren't on the keyboards of most computers.

AutoFormat lines must be checked to make the software replaces the items the writer has indicated on the first two of the screens shown. (The printscreens above illustrate the settings that I used when I was still using Office 2003.)

If you are still writing using Office 2003, you can find numerous sources of more detailed instructions by Googling your questions to Microsoft Word 2003—tutorials.

Open Office Writer

I have never used Open Office Writer, but here is the URL for a very good blog post that demonstrates in detail how to use its autocorrect functions.

> http://openoffice.blogs.com/openoffice/2006/06/autoformats_in_.html

Corel WordPerfect

Via long-ago experience with WordPerfect, I found it very well documented and logically set up to allow a short learning curve for the new user. Corel has created excellent tutorial videos for various recent versions that should prove invaluable for a writer getting started with this software.

http://www.lynda.com/Corel-training-tutorials/110-0.html?category=wordperfect_327

Scrivener

Originally created for Macintosh, Scrivener is not exactly a word processor, although it can be used to keep a writing project integrated, from research to characterization to writing and editing a manuscript. The Mac version differs in looks from its Windows version. Both have autocorrect capabilities, I am told, but I've never gotten so far into the software as to evaluate it. Googling "autocorrect in Scrivener for Mac" or "autocorrect in Scrivener for Windows" will produce extensive lists of references.

No matter what software a writer uses to produce rough drafts, there will be eccentricities that must be accounted for in order to get a book into clean, publishable format. The information in this appendix is intended merely to give pointers toward where the instructions for autocorrecting and spellchecking in various versions of popular software may be located.

I use professional formatters for my self-published books, even my genre fiction which is the simplest of documents to prepare for publication. My recommendations are that others use pros as well, unless they have the particular organized mindset that allows them to dot every "i" and cross every "t." I do not have that type of mindset, just as I don't have the innate talent that would let me create gorgeous cover art.

Self-editing is the function I never shirk. I use the procedures available in Word to make my self-edit easier, but never to substitute for another writing/editing professional's careful read-through. In the long run, that self-edit invariably saves me time and money.

Appendix B –Words Easily Misused/Mistaken

Take a look at the randomly selected samples on the following page. The list is **absolutely** not all-inclusive, but simply a few illustrations of how easily different correctly spelled words may be mistaken for one another. There are thousands, literally, of misspellings that coincidentally spell correct words.

There are at least a few of them that most people either mistype or mistake frequently for other words for other reasons. (You might want to make a checklist and include words you discover should be added to my abbreviated table—and keep it handy for future self-editing.)

Word processors are wonderful...to a point. Spell-checkers can point out or correct words that aren't in their onboard dictionaries, but unless a writer is using the newest aide, **Autocorrect in Context** , which is still in its infancy, that word processor is going to let a good many words pass through that are correctly spelled but may not be what the writer meant to say.

Words that sound the same, or similar
but mean this—

	there	their	they're		
	in that place	of them	they are		
accept	except		aid	aide	
take in	other than		to help	a helper	
ale	ail		allusion	illusion	
alcoholic drink	not well		indirect reference	false appearance	
alter	altar		ate	eight	
to change	table at church		past tense of eat	the number 8	
bare	bear		beat	beet	
uncovered	animal		to strike	a plant	
band	banned		cat	car	
musical group	prohibited		a furry friend	automobile	
condor	condom		eminent	imminent	
a bird	prophylactic		well thought of	soon	
	dam	damp	damn		
	stop for water	not dry	an oath		
	fat	fate	fete		
	overweight	unavoidable	to honor		
	maid	made	may		
	servant	past of make	month		
no	none	no one	nun	one	
opposite yes	not any	no one	religious	the number 1	
pay	pan	par	pain	pane	
give money	to move around	avg golf score	anguish	a window glass	
reimburse	cooking utensil	about right	discomfort		
	zen	zin	zinc		
	a magical place/	zinfandel	elemental metal		

Why do wrong words and misspellings end up in books?

There are several reasons; listed here are the occurrences I believe to be most common.

1.   Writer using dictation software does not enunciate all words clearly enough for the software to transcribe accurately. (I fall under this category, which is why I rarely dictate more than simple text messages—never, ever a novel!)

2.   Writer who types his/her manuscript has a tendency to type words backward, often due to being dyslexic (Example: intends to type "rat", types "tar" instead)

3.   Writer is not a particularly accurate typist, tends to mistake the letter "r" for "t" and end up with the same example as in the one above. (There are other interesting keyboard letter transpositions that end up creating "real" words and thus don't get caught by spell-checkers. Some of these "really wrong" words can make for humorous reading.)

4.   Writer isn't clear as to the spelling of a word, guesses, and is unlucky enough to have hit on another word instead.

5.   After making changes to rough manuscript, writer fails to follow through with related changes, creating new errors that must be fixed.

6.   Writer fails to read the manuscript carefully, beginning to end, after having let it "cool" for as short as a few days and as long as a few months. The cooling-off period tends to lessen the chance that the writer will overlook obvious mistakes.

The writer should take care to ferret out most of these common errors in the self-editing process, so professional editors can concentrate on doing what they are paid to do: editing content, voice and style.

APPENDIX C—STEPS TOWARD A PERFECT MANUSCRIPT

Before beginning to write, an author needs to perform some preliminaries. A chronological list of building a book from concept to finished manuscript follows.

1. **Master the basics of *Self-Editing** for the Writer*, at least in a rudimentary way. This will ease the way as you plan your story, because you will know the potential pitfalls and thus be able to minimize them.

2. **Organize your thoughts** about where your book is going, including character sketches and a rough story progression. (Many books address how to write fiction—short stories, novellas, novels, screenplays and so on. Every writer works from an individual perspective—there are as many ways to outline a potential story as there are writers.)

3. **Write your rough draft**, using self-editing tools to help you avoid making common errors in writing—

misspellings, poor grammar, and so on.

4.   Set the draft aside when you are done—don't try to self-edit it immediately.

5.   **Read the draft, repairing errors** noted by the software as well as those you find while reading **and making revisions** to correct noticeable problems with sentence construction, repetitive information or wording, and story content.

6.   **Re-read the revised text** and verify that the grammar, spelling and word choice are still correct. Many grammar errors stem from a writer's having revised wording but not followed through to make certain that the revised text is still correct as to tense, word choice, and so on.

7.   **Run the software's Find and Replace functions again** to ferret out typos such as duplicate and missing punctuation marks, duplicate blank spaces at the beginnings and endings of paragraphs, and so on.

8.   **Use the Find function** to locate words you frequently misuse, and correct them manually if they are incorrect.

9. **Skim the draft manually** and correct any remaining errors as you see them.

10. **Turn the self-edited draft over to beta readers and/or a professional editor.**

11. When the reader(s) return the draft with their comments, decide whether to make or reject the changes they suggested. Make the revisions you want to accept, and **repeat steps five through nine.**

12. Now your manuscript is ready to be formatted for publication, or to resubmit to your professional editor for further editing. **If it does not require further edit, remove the comments** and format (or submit to formatter) for publication.

Note: All of the steps in self-editing have elements that require human eyes to perform correctly. While software is invaluable, especially when seeking out errors that are difficult to see while doing read-throughs, it cannot substitute for careful reading not only of your rough drafts but also of each revision/rewording you make before arriving at the finished, polished product.

www.ingramcontent.com/pod-product-compliance
Lightning Source LLC
Chambersburg PA
CBHW072012290526
45787CB00013B/759